The Alarming Beauty of the Sky

The Alarming Beauty of the Sky

poems

LESLIE MONSOUR

*For Jeanne — with
greatest pleasure —
Leslie Monsour
4/10/10*

Red Hen Press 🐓 *Los Angeles*

The Alarming Beauty of the Sky

Book design by Michael Vukadinovich
Cover Design by Mark E. Cull

ISBN: 1-59709-006-9
Library of Congress Catalog Card Number: 2005900678

Published by Red Hen Press

The City of Los Angeles Cultural Affairs Department, California Arts
Council, Los Angeles County Arts Commission and National Endowment
for the Arts partially support Red Hen Press.

First Edition

In memory of my mother,

Margaret Browning,

"Hollywood's Youngest Poet"

Acknowledgments

Journals:
Birmingham Poetry Review: "The Natural World," "Rainy Eclipse," "The Memory of Abortion Unexpectedly Returns" ; *Hellas:* "Looking for Alligators Near Kennedy Space Center," "Metamorphosis" ; *The Lyric:* "The Peach Tree" ; *The Plum Review:* "Parking Lot," "Middle Age" ; *Fourteen Hills:* "Second Honeymoon" ; *Able Muse:* "Film Noir," "Reading Robert Frost. . . ," "A Feminine Riposte . . ." ; *Poetry:* "Nimis Compos Mentis ," "Travel Plans," "Sightseers," "Dividing China" ; *The Dark Horse:* "My Old Man, Picking Lemons," "The Old Capitalist"; *The Edge City Review:* "The Bachelor"; *The Formalist:* "The Education of a Poet"; *Pivot:* "Illusion of Loss," "I Felt the Tree Go Bare," "The Snail in the Marigold," "Odyssey," ; "Keeping Up Appearances"; *Schuylkill Valley Journal of the Arts:* "Fifties Music," "Time + Distance"— Jim Marinell Grand Poetry Prize Winner (reprinted from *Travel Plans* R. L. Barth Press, 2001)

Anthologies:
A Formal Feeling Comes. Poems in Form by Contemporary Women ed. Annie Finch. Story Line Press, 1994 ("Emily's Words," "Metamorphosis," "Sweeping") *Visiting Emily: Contemporary Poems Inspired by the Life and Work of Emily Dickinson* eds. Thom Tammaro, Sheila Coghill. University of Iowa Press, 2000 ("Emily's Words") *New Formalist Poets of the American West* ed. April Lindner. Boise State University Press, 2001 ("Emily's Words," "Parking Lot") *Northern Music. Poems about and Inspired by Glenn Gould* ed. J.D. Smith. John Gordon Burke Publisher, Inc., 2001 ("The Last Concert") *California Poetry from the Gold Rush to the Present* eds. Dana Gioia, Chryss Yost, Jack Hicks. Heydey Books, 2003 ("Parking Lot," "Nimis Compos Mentis")

Chapbooks:
Earth's Beauty, Desire, & Loss. Robert L. Barth Press. 1998 *Indelibility.* Aralia Press. 1999 *Travel Plans.* Robert L. Barth Press. 2001

Contents

I

Travel Plans 13

The Natural World 14

Still Life with Insects 15

Sightseers 16

The Ocean May Have Been the
    Last Thing She Saw 17

Illusion of Loss 18

My Old Man, Picking Lemons 19

The Suddenness of the Past 20

Augury 21

Returning Home 22

Middle Age 23

II

The Snail in the Marigold 27

Desert Prayer 28

The Peach Tree 29

Calla Lilies 30

Rainy Eclipse 31

Looking Back over San Marcos Pass 32

Indelibility 33

Metamorphosis 34

On Finding a Salamander
    in the Hollywood Hills 35

Keeping Up Appearances 36

Looking for Alligators near
    Kennedy Space Center 37

The Burrowing Bees 38

Hotel Balcony 40

III

Time + Distance   43

Summer Tankas   44

The Stream at Jackass Meadow   45

I Felt the Tree Go Bare   46

Green   47

Fifties Music   48

Second Honeymoon   49

Nimis Compos Mentis   50

The Pool   52

Lothario   53

This Kiss   54

The Bachelor   55

IV

Odyssey   59

The Last Concert   60

Mary Cassatt. Two Studies   61

The Train Bearer   63

Fifteen   64

The Outfielder   65

Shell   66

The Memory of Abortion
     Unexpectedly Returns   67

Film Noir   68

Lake Arrowhead   69

Northridge, 1952: A Mother Looks
     for Her Children   70

Conundrum   72

V

To the Poet Who Thinks
   I Praise Promiscuously   75
The Education of a Poet   76
Letter to Philip Larkin   77
A Feminine Riposte
   to X.J. Kennedy   80
Thoughts while Reading Robert
   Frost on New Year's Day in Idaho   81
On Hearing Gwendolyn Brooks   82
Emily's Words   83
Sweeping   84
The Old Capitalist   85
Dividing China   86
Parking Lot   87

I

Travel Plans

The pepper tree spilled round us from its source,
and took a lumpish this-way, that-way course,
while dangling hopeful sprays of cinnabar.
You couldn't rest against the grizzled trunk;
its bulby hump, its knurled and craggy scar,
forced you to lean your weight on me instead.
The two of us were just a little drunk,
and sipped the sun-warmed wine to make us bold.

"I'd like to go to Mexico," you said,
"with you, someday, before we're too damn old,"
while in the sky an airplane's vapor trail
politely licked its seal across the sun.
We watched the growing, tantalizing tail,
until it matter-of-factly came undone.

The Natural World

Just outside the study window,
Gazing down where vines and brush
Embramble frozen earth, a slow
And shrugging motion, like a push

Or something digging, caught our stare.
One raccoon, as dark as slate,
Worked his partner, she a fair
And richly furred, reluctant mate,

Both unaware they entertained
Two who watched self-consciously.
And when the gray mass broke and strained
Apart, we shared a sip of tea

And saw them spill beyond our view
As light blue streaks fell on the bay,
As if the natural world and we
Had low and sudden things to say.

Still Life with Insects

The katydids are clicking in the dust.
I once compared them to Kandinsky's green,
When one came in the kitchen, and we watched
Its strutting legs complexly climb the screen.

Afterwards, I went to the museum,
And bought a postcard, showing what I meant
About the open-heartedness of colors
(Time seemed much slower then, and lighter spent).

Today a blue-black wasp works arduously.
It scoops a gravel nursery lined with dung,
Abducts and seals within, a sleeping spider—
An incubator-wet nurse for its young.

This happens in the patio while I light
A smoke; my breath, exhaled, shifts with the breeze,
Uncertainly away . . . and back to me.
The evening haze is lingering in the trees

And in the pathless canyon. Near my foot
A silver bee hoards pollen in its hole—
While night, the other shoe, falls on us all
With ash-gray mothwings pressed against its sole.

Sightseers

A string of pelicans in gliding file
Traversed the setting sun. We watched awhile
Before the captain shared an observation:
"The pelicans die early, from starvation.
They waste ashore, unable to take flight;
They haven't lost their wings, they've lost their sight.
The reason they go blind is said to be
The force with which they plunge into the sea
To nab their catch; it massacres their eyes."

Hard nature made them rash instead of wise.
They threaded to a point. We kept our eyes on
Their drift, above the gaudy-hued horizon,
Where sun's last glimmer sipped the darkening tide,
And night awaited, opulently eyed.

The Ocean May Have Been the Last Thing She Saw

In line at the marina liquor store,
She'd grip the fifth of vodka like an oar,
Then row around in circles half the night,
And raise, with her Atlantic-colored eyes,
A thousand toasts to the impervious skies.

She liked to drink until she had to squint
To see one moon above the reef, and spent
Her days marooned on a chaise longue with white,
Redundant waves and shipwrecked suns. Now gulls
And hungry cormorants huddle in the shoals,

Where seahorse babies curl around the grasses
And broken seashells mingle with her ashes.

Illusion of Loss

Departing ships grow small and melt away
From those on shore who weep and watch them go;
But ships loom large as life beyond the bay,
As those on board who make the voyage know.

My Old Man, Picking Lemons

He brastles through the bushes, tugging hard
at unripe fruit that won't let go. His yard
consists of pavement, pool, and citrus trees.

Palm Springs has been so awfully hot and dry,
the sparrows have to hatch before they fry.
It is one hundred seventeen degrees.

The branch rips from the stem and rocks the boughs.
He almost loses balance, whoops, and throws
the lemon, like some tumorous disease,

into a market bag. The violence
makes juicy, ready ones above the fence
drop on the neighbor's side, which does not please

my father, steadily at loggerheads
with everything around him, as he treads
his narrow, gravelled property. No breeze

relieves his dusty grove, no hope of joy.
He grunts and stoops, and, toppling, cries, "Oh, boy,"
then swears and knocks the pebbles from his knees.

The pool's too warm mid-day, and much too shallow
For cooling off. I take the bag of yellow
harvest, a poke of tragicomedies,
and tell my father, "Thanks," and get my keys.

The Suddenness of the Past

I hit a hummingbird today, while driving
To the commencement of my oldest son.
I saw its hair-slim beak, its pinpoint, living
Eye. It popped against the windshield and was gone.

I pushed ahead, not actually seeing
Much else beyond the radiating throw
Of red across the glass, a proof of being,
Caught in its wherenesses, a smear of now,

The way my heart is streaked with iridescent-
Feathered reminders, tiny-throated fears.
I watch my son stand clearly in the present,
Unflinching, like the emerald silk he wears.

Augury

for John Rechy

Transfixed by autumn sun's retreating blaze,
we stop to watch a pair of red-tailed hawks.
In skyward suit, commingling in the haze,

they consummate, secure, above the rocks.
Mid-path, we come across a fallen feather;
it imitates our tense tranquillity,

our eccentricity of past restraint.
Collecting it, I can't determine whether
this dusty emblem of fidelity

is noble, dignified . . . or merely quaint.

Returning Home

The whispers of the house are not our own;
They're of our absence, air unbreathed, dead moths.
It's musty here. Our old thoughts stretch and yawn
Like wakened dogs. We start where we left off,

Go for a walk, reclaim familiar streets,
Bring in the customary flowers, fill
The laundry basket, rest on unchanged sheets,
Pull dandelions by twilight, sort the mail.

From far away, the usual doors slam tight,
And nothing seems to alter, till a breath
Of jasmine sweetly stealing through the night
Is beautiful enough. It's all that's left

Of wonderment, entangled in the hedge,
Beside the frankness of the window's dust,
The moonlit candor of its peeling ledge,
The old wood rotting, as, of course, it must.

Middle Age

The morning paper slaps the driveway's face
And brings the wincing blush of dawn. A brace

Of shrewd and ink-stained, unsubjective crows
Are measuring and editing our street,
While I review the paleness of my feet
And curl an edge of carpet with my toes.

An oily dimness floods the hand-loomed floor.
It comprehends the corners, knows the hall
The way a shadow understands a wall.
I mark the rhythm of your muffled snore

And almost envy how you navigate
Your dark and shuddering forehead through a dream.
The ebbing night and swelling morning seem
To touch each other as they hesitate,

And light invades the room—the sun is strong,
The fractures in the ceiling, wide and long.

II

The Snail in the Marigold

I watched, when planting marigolds,
Their colors all afire,
A gorged snail suck amid the folds,
Unfurling with desire—

Its slick and gleaming trail of pleasure
Oozing out behind;
Its rapturous head in worldly leisure,
Oblivious, petal-blind.

The broken bud looked jubilant,
Enravished, vibrant, real,
Infusing animal and plant
With sybaritic zeal.

This seeming drive to be consumed
As wood lit in a stove,
Must be the lavishest, most doomed,
And pure of earthly love.

Come, celebrate the appetite
No science can control,
The wild, ingenious, slippery blight
That incarnates the soul.

Desert Prayer

Prayer is the contemplation of the facts of life from the highest point of view.

—Emerson

A gleaming granite ocean, bold as light
and strewn with bright, coarse stuff—a million suns,
the shells of ancient seas and modern guns—
the grand Mojave disappears at night,

its long and open syllable of air,
the breath of all that lives and dies out there.

Surrounded by the silent sprawl of sage,
I see the stark indifference of its grace,
the glare of stillness on its living face;
I feel the hope-free weight of rockbound age,

and for an instant, heaven-reaching joy,
at poppies pushing through the wind-cracked clay.

The sudden dive when hawk and eagle soar,
is sky's collaboration with the land.
Here, eye-like burrows, socketed in sand,
surrender truth from earth's consenting floor;

here, timorous hearts keep time in fur and bone.
I know the count; their thumping is my own.

The Peach Tree

It's hot, and we have more than we can eat.
But Mother, in her unlit room, her feet
All dry and bed-chapped, doesn't want a bit
Of food. She only likes to have me sit
Beside her and squeeze Jergens on her toes,
Then rub until her eyes begin to close.

The peach tree, open-armed and in its prime,
Is much too full of ripened fruit to climb.
We give each other boosts to squeeze the skins
And bite into the soft ones, bathe our chins
With bright, warm juice. (That strong and healthy tree
Was like a universe of hope for me).

At night we go inside. We can't do more
Than softly say goodnight and close her door,
And watch "The Twilight Zone" in black and white.
The heavens turn, I see the burning light,
And hear the stars that drop and die up there
Like peaches falling in hot summer air.

Calla Lilies

The Mayans plant their lilies in the corn,
And in the clay along the streams and marshes.
The women march to market under long
And sturdy stems that look like gathered guns.
Their feet are bare on paths of mud, their daughters
Keep step behind them, shouldering the flowers
Like land-bound saints with blossom wings and pollen
Halos sifting down obsidian braids.
Their pilgrim rhythm whispers in the leaves
That blaze, full-blooded green, like shields and banners.
The lamb-white lilies openly reveal
A thrust of yolk-bright weapons, aimed and loaded,
So earth will not forget to make more flowers.

Rainy Eclipse

for Mario and Martha Joy Gottfried
Valle de Bravo, Mexico. July 11, 1991

A starling, like a piece of chipped basalt,
Swerves high above the dark volcano, quiet
As ash across the chimney-colored basin
Of sky, the plug pulled out and all the light

Gone up the hole. I have an icy gulp
Of cola-flavored Bacardí. Its brown,
Sweet taste is all that glows. The black and sudden
Moon lasts seven minutes. Back in town,

Where blackbirds curse the lake along the shore,
Some boys hold up a lifeless fish to blame
The sky for scaring it to death. They say
The water's been bewitched, it's not the same.

I pass a man outside the *pulquería.*
He's stony, like a saint without a shrine,
Propped up against the chipped, celestial wall.
I love the way his shadow blends with mine.

Looking Back over San Marcos Pass

Each time I leave, the magpies scoot aside.
They're always there, patrolling in the drive,
As business-like as judges, black and white.

This may well be the most alone I've felt,
The most engulfed in nothing (but a view).
A universe as stunning as this gorge,

As deep and silent, opens up between us.
The highway climbs, and I look back to see
The drought-exposed terrain of Lake Cachuma's

Palomino shore. That's when I drop
Into the straightaway where last September
I flew past squadrons of tarantulas

Roadside at dusk like pirates making land;
And, once, a squandered heap of gunny sacks
Turned out to be the body of a puma.

But now the air is pitched with bats, and though
The humpback moon is flanking me, reflecting
A landscape full of blunders and intrusions,

I'm comforted by how you offered me
Some serpentine you picked up from the ground
—Unyielding, thaw-proof stone—and how I pressed

It, earth-cool in my palm, and made it warm.

Indelibility

A whistle in the palm outside my window
Announced a yellow warbler perched there like
A feathered spark, a sun-flake with a pinto
Wingflash. I saw it flicker, burn, then spike
The air in take-off. Gone. And yet, the bird
Remains. The world outside is not the same,
With shifting shadows, air and time disturbed;
But in my mind is locked the singing flame.

Metamorphosis

The hammock was a blue cocoon,
And I, its seeing worm,
A fading tune, a crescent moon,
The threads about me, firm.

I fell into a purr of sleep
Amid the greeny glint,
The dewy weep, the leafy sweep
Of myrtle and of mint.

And while I slept, the tree went round
In galaxies of shade,
Till every pound and every sound
Were blissfully unmade,

And I was scattered everywhere
As nothing in no place;
No web of air, no net of care,
No earth, no tree, no face.

On Finding a Salamander in the Hollywood Hills

Into deep shade a salamander crept.
It curled its body there, and moistly slept,
Till I removed an old agave pot.

The mire convulsed in little specks of blue.
A shape was generated from the stew,
As if the mud had conjured up a thought.

I scooped it up and cupped it in my palm.
It flashed its bolting tongue, stayed boldly calm,
Its aspic flesh congealing in a knot

Of ancient blood, the ripened afterbirth
Of roses, springing from the fabled earth,
Preposterous, like something time forgot.

Across the laurel chaparral and oak,
The shadows shrank, the season smelled of smoke.
The salamander, so the myth is taught,

Can withstand fire. With fierce, bituminous stare,
The way a dying star dims with a flare,
It blinked away the noonday sun's white-hot

And airy universe of bees and birds
And poets prospering on weightless words,
Then crawled back to its ponderous realm of rot,
Pinning me like a magnet to the spot.

Keeping Up Appearances

Down at the endangered species park
We watch from windowed trams
The marvellous heirs of Noah's ark,
And wave our oriflammes.

The keepers drag a side of beef
Behind a Chevrolet
While lions suspend their disbelief
And chase the vulgar prey.

The drowsy tigers, overfed,
Too fat to bolt or rage,
Go poker-faced as they are led
Inside a sterile cage.

They lick off patches of their fur
In apathetic bliss,
With loathing in each lambent purr,
And hope in every hiss.

Looking for Alligators near Kennedy Space Center

The air is still until a catfish clangs
The swampy surface like a dirty bell

And breaks the spell between the elements.
At well-considered distances, the heron

And ibis wade, unrushing, noiseless, keen.
Abruptly, near our feet, a flat-shelled turtle

Dives under, while an osprey's liquid cry
Intensifies the mangroves, and behind us

The armadillos occupy the reeds.
The alligator's been there all along,

A horizontal bargain with the shore:
The famous smile, the lifted, level head—

A ledge with teeth. Its open eye blinks once.
A statue of itself, a resolute

And stationary universe, it watches,
Holding fast, resisting evolution.

Again, a long, slow blink, and we, like moons,
Revolve with sunhats and binoculars.

The Burrowing Bees

I prize their wild and solitary charm
Of being. They serve no queen, and thrive
   Without conforming to the ritual and swarm
Of the industrious, honey-brewing hive.

Two weeks ago, the patio gave birth
To mounds of dirt where pavement cracked and lent
   A gritty opportunity to sound the earth.
They took a sunny corner of cement

Where heat starts early, lasting all the day.
First five or six, now several dozen zip
   Around in admirable disorder; drones relay
In restless idleness, while females slip

Like rain into their rocky subdivision,
Encrusted with the bullion of their toil,
   And, crouched among them, I rejoice in the precision
With which they hang midair, dissolve in soil.

They growl like dainty bullets, whipping, shooting
About my feet. I shift to find a spot
   Less near their sandy rings, the funneled cells for brooding,
Riddled beneath the fragrant bergamot.

At last, the males, converging, take the floor,
And, ravishing their mates in silvery blazes,
   Like frenzied tumbleweeds, they rollick, three and four,
With heads and abdomens in teeming mazes.

Their progeny is their preoccupation;
And time exists to see that life occurs
    In sequence: the crucial splicing of a generation,
The fertile spring each larvaed heir ensures.

At dusk, the cooling stones grow still again.
The world depends upon the sleeping bees—
    Their chambered hymn,
        the last clear thought inside God's brain—
Accompanied by distant piano keys.

Hotel Balcony

This crib is bolted firmly to the wall.
From here I watch the sea, its shades of green,
And save the junebugs crashing on the screen
From dying upside down. With stupored crawl,
And plodding flight, they make fine toys, as psalms
Break loose from sparrows passing by. I glance
At people milling home and think of ants,
Then nod at someone leaning on his palms
Across from me, who stares at something lost
The way we gaze from windows of a train
At places we won't ever see again;
And life unwinds, as if it had been tossed
Like a "Surprise Ball" from our place of birth,
Unwrapping trinket glimpses of the earth.

III

Time + Distance

The tea you pour is black and strong.
It doesn't taste like tea to me;
I must have been away too long.

It isn't jasmine, spice, oolong;
It tastes like an apology—
This tea you pour, so black and strong.

Where's that old fork with the bent prong?
What happened to the hemlock tree?
Have I really been gone that long?

I think I hear the saddest song;
It has no words, no tune, no key.
The tea you pour is black and strong.

You're careful to say nothing wrong,
You seem too eager to agree...
Yes, I've been travelling far and long,

And now it's clear, I don't belong.
I watch you sash your robe, as we
sit, sipping tea that's black and strong.
I went away too far, too long.

Summer Tankas

THE TOMATOES HAVE NOT BEEN HAPPY THIS YEAR
They're tall and thin as
shy girls. The pale buds wither
and come to nothing,
falling in brown clumps, like failed
poems strewn about the desk.

TOURISTS
Driving, I notice
a sunburned couple who've stopped
to admire the plants
in front of a nondescript
building I pass every day.

PURPOSE & BEER
I drain a pitcher,
watch the sun rust in the sea,
and think about You.
The lone gull and I ask, "Why,
really, have You brought us here?"

OPEN WINDOW
Surprise rain begins.
Drops tap out their destinies.
Shades of green deepen.
We float on the couch and let
air's mute currents wash our skin.

The Stream at Jackass Meadow
for John

Along the muddy bank where logs
Lay stretched, the water held its breath
While insects swooped to plant their eggs.
You strung the fish on severed twigs
That threaded through the gill and mouth;
We carried them along the path,
Their bodies curling, nearing death.

With eyes moon-colored, dreamless, blank,
Each rainbow gaped in ebbing froth,
And weakly slapped against the sink,
Inhaling air, their cruel drink—
While at the screen, a green-eyed moth,
The moon above it, to the south,
Reduced its wings to ragged cloth.

All night we lay next to the flame,
Our bones and flesh together sliding,
Like the river slowly gliding
Across smooth stones. The moon was fading
Behind the narrow pines, or hiding
Its sated belly, like a dream,
Drawn down into the fish-filled stream.

I Felt the Tree Go Bare

Imagining the trees were evergreen,
Alone we lay for hours and caressed
Each other, lost, behind his house, unseen.

The swooning boughs that sheltered us grew lean.
What fall would do to us, I never guessed,
Or what the coldness in the ground could mean.

For now there is no shade, no place to rest,
No filtered light, all dappled and serene;
No leaf remains, no trace of any nest.

I felt the tree go bare inside my breast.

Green

This is the green of kissing on the lawn,
Dichondra stains and promises at dawn,

Of ivy, mint and fern, profuse oxalis—
This green is not of *mal-de-mer* or malice

Or wolf-is-at-the-door-and-wants-a-date,
But yearling nibbling clover at my gate;

Nasturtium leaves and take me to the fair,
This green is how he breathes into my hair,

And how his lashes sweetly droop in sleep
Like mossy glens where willow shadows creep.

This green is pepper trees and hide-and-seek;
This green has asked to marry me next week.

I'll have this green—I'll have it now, and fast.
It's full of life—it isn't going to last.

Fifties Music

While women sip their daiquiries by the pool,
and men blow smoke into the jacarandas,
the radio plays "Fly Me to the Moon."

A child nearby, on finding a dead bee,
conducts its funeral in petunia beds,
as ants are trying to amputate a wing.

But even though the bee seems dead, it stings
her fiercely on the palm, and dies again.
She studies her small hand in disbelief.

Some fathers offer ice cubes from their highballs,
the station plays "Volare," and the bee
swings up to heaven on its single wing.

Second Honeymoon

Whales come here every year to mate and breed.
They nose and bite in the intimate currents, rolling
and moaning as if dying. My whiskied thoughts
are brown and lurching. Sitting near you, I'm
unable to appraise our distance.

The crickets noodle from a distant hedge
beneath the fullest moon. The night is boring.
A palm looms like a lunatic. No breeze
bestirs its shape—except a rat-like rustle
in its dark heart. Up north, some whales are stranded.
I dream I hear them, trapped beneath the ice.

Nimis Compos Mentis

The paper table cloth was tastefully bleak,
The misty morning light shone on his cheek,
And made him look alone and masculine.

He talked of Seneca and bad translations,
Of modern critics' lightweight observations;
A bread crumb rested sweetly on his chin.

Behind him, through the glass, the ocean's heave
Uncurled against the sand, beside his sleeve,
As Eros aimed his toxic javelin.

I ducked out of the way to no avail;
It glanced my flesh, injecting quite a cocktail
That blurred my sight and gave my head a spin—

Never mind the coffee we were drinking,
Whatever I said was not what I was thinking:
I wanted to become his mandolin,

And lie across his lap, a dainty lute,
And sing to him and feed him ripened fruit,
While light upon the sea turned opaline.

Instead, this conversation about art
And formal education—God, he's smart!
Such rationality should be a sin.

The hour was up, he had to run, of course;
A handshake and a peck of shy remorse—
Outside, the sea was gray and dull as tin;
It ruled the shore with tedious discipline.

The Pool

A male jay from the rubber plant
Flew down where I sat waiting
For you to come and swim with me.
He eyed the blades of grass,

Then quietly from roots of sod,
Plucked out an earth-clad worm,
With self-sufficient certainty,
And jaunty heedlessness.

The worm was swallowed, dirt and all;
The sated creature left.
I closed the book I hadn't read,
Prepared to swim alone.

The sun was branded on the pool—
I still expected you.
You have a way of showing up
Just like that hungry bird;

You know exactly what to do—
And I'm the yielding lawn.
You find the writhing worm in me
That moves and dies for you.

The surface shattered with my dive
Into the pool's deep roar;
The water might have been the sky,
Clear to the blurry floor.

Lothario

Today he cups his hands into a heart,
Unable to hold anything but air.
Desire, like ocean, seeps between his palms;
He sees reflections of it everywhere.

Tonight he sprouts a pair of flashy wings,
But only sets the lantern as his goal
(It's warmer than the moon, and near). Take care,
My love, the blinded mothworm of his soul
Will nibble hungrily, for that's his art:
To spoil the fleecy vestment of your heart.

This Kiss

This kiss is growing less and less platonic.
What tasted plain is starting to taste sweet—
And, yes, I'll have another gin and tonic

To calm my nervous hands and this demonic
Voracity each time we part or meet;
This kiss is growing less and less platonic.

Our eyes have started flashing supersonic
Monitions, lest we be inclined to cheat—
And, yes, I'll have another gin and tonic.

I'll try to countermand my histrionic
Urges to go swooning at your feet;
This kiss is growing less and less platonic,

I wish I felt a little less sardonic
Because of age. Still, let's turn up the heat—
And, yes, I'll have another gin and tonic;

Perhaps it will establish a harmonic
Convergence to my heart's unnerving beat.
This kiss is growing less and less platonic,
And, yes, I'll have another gin and tonic.

The Bachelor

No family pictures on the wall, no books,
      A drafting desk, a travel magazine;
No children, one divorce, a satellite dish—
      A cold, efficient exercise machine,

And in the corner with the firewood, stacks
      Of videos. The fridge comes with "lite" beer
And non-fat milk for the granola stored
      In jars. I've looked, but there's no sugar here.

Platoons of running shoes camp by the door;
      His Boston fern, neglected, pays the price;
His one unfriendly cat purposefully saunters
      Across the threshold, searching hard for mice.

As he begins to age, and his gray beard
      Inaugurates the thinning of his hair,
He'll pale with each sensation in his chest,
      Each flutter, every pain and numbness there—

      No cardiologist, nor any chart
      Will ever find the trouble with his heart.

IV

Odyssey

A young explorer sails his market cart
Down aisles of "sell by" dates and cleaning potions.
With wild surmise, this stout little Cortez
Surveys the bar-coded and shrink-wrapped oceans.

His nanny buys him plastic toys and bon bons.
Already, his arcadia's been explored
To death and sweetened artificially.
He'll cross the long-houred seas of youth ignored.

A satellite dish will be his northern star.
A couch will be the vessel for his journeys.
He'll navigate with joystick and remote,
His fortune gone to custody attorneys.

The Last Concert
for Glenn Gould

Before he plays, he fills the bathroom basin
with birthwarm water for his room-chilled hands.
The way he floats them, they could be his child;
they have his seriousness, and there's his face in
their grasp, which heaven won't exceed. He stands
flexing off tension, bathes his wrists with mild
affection, almost with a father's pride.
He is their master as they're towelled, and such
demanding expectation he'll impart,
when fingers upon ivories collide
in strain-resolving fugue, they'll lightly touch
the pulse of love's severe, exacting heart.

Mary Cassatt. Two Studies

I. PATIENCE
[After "Young Thomas and His Mother"—pastel]

She props him on the couch after his nap.
He's damp and warm. He whimpers, will she let
Him see her necklace? Afternoons are wet
And heavy since July. He finds her lap
Too sweltering, her dress does not feel nice
Against his skin. He much prefers the cold
Metallic chain, the locket made of gold.
She sniffs his tender arm, that sweet, rare spice.

He's glad Papá has gone away for now—
Mamá reclines her head and pays no heed
To passing time, dexterity or speed.
Unlike Papá's "Let **me. I'll** show you how,"
She quietly lets him try. The halves divide
A little world with ticking hands inside.

II. THE ENVELOPE

[after "The Letter"—color print with drypoint and aquatint]

Olivia's at her desk and vainly tries
To end a letter carefully begun,
Inviting him (nerves flash behind her eyes)
To come to tea next week at half-past one.
The wallpaper creates a little park,
A curling hedge of safe, ungiving thought.
Her dampened brow knits rows of question marks
Entwined with wisps of hair. Her throat grows hot

At sealing up the letter with her tongue—
So intimate an act will never do.
And yet she doesn't like to keep a sponge,
Endures, instead, the pungent taste of glue.
She lays the letter down upon the blotter
And smooths her bodice, while her throat grows hotter.

The Train Bearer

I hear the march begin and see the bride
Ascend the concrete steps, her frothy train
Like water flowing up a mountainside,

Pursuing her; an eerie, rising rain,
Sucked from the doorway's threshold to the eaves—
A spill of blood pulled back inside the vein.

Out here, a sycamore is dropping leaves.
They're drifting down to earth like scarecrow gloves,
And clouds have rolled across the sky in sleeves

That magically produce a flock of doves.
The roots have pushed the sidewalk full of cracks,
And I am wondering if she fears or loves

The man inside. I smell the candle wax.
The sickly glow transforms her brilliant lace,
And plaster saints stare down from wooden racks.

The groom prepares to take the father's place.

Fifteen

The boys who fled my father's house in fear
Of what his wrath would cost them if he found
Them nibbling slowly at his daughter's ear,
Would vanish out the back without a sound,
And glide just like the shadow of a crow,
To wait beside the elm tree in the snow.

Something quite deadly rumbled in his voice.
He sniffed the air as if he knew the scent
Of teenage boys, and asked, "What was that noise?"
Then I'd pretend to not know what he meant,
Stand mutely by, my heart immense with dread,
As Father set the traps and went to bed.

The Outfielder

There's Jesse, planted in left field,
a sapling in the burning sun.
He looks so small and far away.
A batter wields a torch-like bat

above home plate, then swings and hits
a solid swack, while everyone
thinks: Homer! Panic hits the dugout
floor. The fielders hurry south,

and Jesse, running backwards, face
to sky, arms reaching, lifts the leather
mitt, a hatchling's open beak.
The ball drops into sight an instant,

then slips into the gullet of
his glove, while heaven glows as if
it swallowed its own blaze. The dust
looks more like smoke as he runs in,

and, slowing at the chain-link wire,
to cheers displays the smothered fire.

Shell

The station where I buy my gas
Has pigeons roosting in the beams
Above the self-serve pumps. Below
Fluorescent lights that glow all night, I see
The parents dozing near their quaking nests.

The moon, a dime in nighttime's shoe,
Shines down on wires connecting us—
Metal and gas, feathers and blood—
The heavy, shuddering lot of us, like some
Forgotten egg, beneath Orion's sword.

The Memory of Abortion Unexpectedly Returns

The sun has trailed its negligee across
The pinkened threshold of the globe and left
Behind a blue-gray edge around the window.
Selecting silken undies from a drawer,
She thinks of loneliness and hummingbirds.

A violet-crowned one sometimes comes to perch
In solitude against the evening sky;
It's sitting there right now, in plainest view,
Digesting nectar, waiting for the night
To settle. Suddenly it breaks away,

A tiny, falling glow she can't retrieve—
Unlike the camisole forever sliding
Off of the lacquered bedpost to the floor—
As light as ashes, light as sighs; a small,
Bright, sleeping bird that dies and dies and dies.

Film Noir

A pair of eyes blink dimly in despair;
Downstairs, a hallway clock is pulsing hard
To amplify the sense of keeping guard
Against the thing that might strike any time,
As midnight's throbbing doom begins to chime.

The bedmate is a guiltless, unlit shape,
Whose presence further serves to block escape.
A pair of eyes blink dimly in despair,
While that caught face, whose sinking heart I share,
Burns isolately in the light-drained air.

Lake Arrowhead

Beneath the dock she supplely crouches,
her form, a young amphibian's.
Earth's fragrant oxygen arises

with every slender beam of breath.
It's easy to conceive a ribbon
of twitching tadpole tail inside

her polka-dotted swimsuit, while
she roots the shore with wise, pink fingers,
extracting skins of dragonflies,

the crystal slippers left behind
of cast-off, primal naiad shapes.
She basks amid duck-noozled mire

of lakeweed sump, and gazes at
her human mother, who's about
to snap a photo in the slanting

auroral flood. But it's the mud
that sings to her; the dear, sweet mud
that plants its kisses on her heels,

and proudly lifts her to the sun.

Northridge, 1952:
A Mother Looks for Her Children

They may have crossed the cornfield
and gone into the butcher's
to see the rabbits twitch...

but could they stand the stubble
on their bare feet? She wondered.
Perhaps in the tall grasses,

playing at hide-and-seek;
or else inside the wash shed,
cranking hapless earwigs

through the laundry wringer . . .
or drowning the black widows
that nest within the tub;

or with the Larson boys,
reciting dirty words?
She listens for their glee.

Perhaps just down the road,
feasting on Cheerios
with Flash, the old coonhound;

or peering through the reeking
oleander hedge
into Mad Gertie's yard.

Then Larson in his Plymouth
stops by to see how many
fresh eggs she'll want this week,

just as a sonic boom
sends cats up sugar pines,
and children running home.

Conundrum

As soon as I say now,
it's then; and here is barely
here an instant till
it's there, where now has been.
For here escapes from now,
And when now catches up
to here, it is nowhere.

V

To the Poet Who Thinks I Praise Promiscuously
for Dick Davis

You're right, I like to compliment my friends,
And I have sometimes been one who pretends
To like things when I don't. Haven't we all?
My mother taught two lessons I recall:
Politeness breeds persuasibility;
Say nothing if it risks hostility
Or pain.
       But now you call it cowardice
And insincerity, a soulless kiss
Intended to dismiss a date and close
The door, a phony smile, a languid pose.
Dear friend, I'm honest, but I have a heart.
It feels all wrong to criticize the art
Of those I prize. Blind caring reassures.
Or does it reek of childhood? Mine, or yours?

The Education of a Poet

Her pencil poised, she's ready to create,
Then listens to her mind's perverse debate
On whether what she does serves any use;
And that is all she needs for an excuse
To spend all afternoon and half the night
Enjoying poems other people write.

Letter to Philip Larkin

I want a form that's big enough to swim in,
And talk on any subject that I choose.
         —Auden: *Letter to Lord Byron*

A balmy night in hills above L.A.,
    A callow century's fifteenth full moon,
A spread of vegetarian buffet,
    A group prepared to revel and commune—
    Until, " 'I just think it will happen, soon',",
The pessimistic close of "Going, Going",
Was spoke, and woe, along with wine, was flowing.

And so, dear Larkin, did our spirits fade,
    Despite night-blooming jasmine stealing in
On zephyrs weaving through the open shade.
    The 'cast of crooks and tarts' you feared would win,
    And bury us in greeds up to our chin,
Is thriving, as is rampant, unread verse,
Which is, as each year passes, getting worse.

A distant firetruck slurred a slow lament,
    And in its wake, coyotes howled and yipped,
As if to mock their own predicament.
    "Poor devils," someone said. Another quipped,
    "They sound as if they've lost their souls," and sipped
The last remains of doleful Beaujolais.
Brandy, uncorked, persuaded us to stay.

Great Satchmo brought us bliss from a CD,
            And held us in a thrall of Larkin lore.
We're all to blame; we all, to some degree,
            Mess earth about, chuck filth, and scream for more.
            We have our share of days. What are days for?
We toasted your despair by candle light,
While moonlit palm fronds glittered in the night.

A grapefruit fell and skidded off the tiles.
            "Most things may never happen; that one will,"
I said, to moody laughs and nodding smiles.
            The trumpet and the brandy fought the chill
            That folded with the fog over the hill
Above the patio. Homes are so sad:
Bank calendars, the realtor's memo pad,

Sprinklers that spit on every weed-whacked lawn.
            We haven't grown more kind while we've had time,
And mums and dads keep fucking up their spawn.
            We escape by car, and from the highway's climb,
            We see the wide Pacific: sleek, sublime—
The coastal shelf that deepens with suspense—
Its abalone blue, pristine, intense.

Intensely sad, you'd say, like choirs of money.
　　　How much do rich shits fork out for this view?
Who cares how many days a year are sunny,
　　　When, seismically, destruction's overdue?
　　　Wherever home is now, we're glad you knew
The pleasure of employing artful breath
In loathing life, and loathing, harder, death.

Note: The Larkin poems referred to are: Going, Going; Days; Aubade; Home Is So Sad; The Mower; This Be the Verse; Money

Also referred to is Philip Larkin's career as a jazz critic, and his great admiration for Louis Armstrong.

A Feminine Riposte to X.J. Kennedy

Meter
Is the thrust rest thrust of loins and peter
And rhyme,
To come at the same time.
—from "Two Views of Rhyme and Meter"

Measure
Is the stress unstress of want and pleasure;
And rhyme,
To do it one more time.

Thoughts While Reading Robert Frost on New Year's Day in Idaho

*(A church with a crooked belfry stands in Bellevue,
Idaho, just south of Hailey, where Ezra Pound was born,
and Ketchum, where Ernest Hemingway shot himself).*

In Hailey, north of Bellevue's misshaped belfry,
A child with cantos crouching in his head
Left ponderous snowtracks as he tugged his sled
Across the years to die in Italy,
In exile with his famed non-metric pound
Of hate. While in the state where Ez was born,
Things went awry in Ernest one lead dawn,
The Big Wood's splashroar drowning every sound,
Until the shot, which friends and family said
Was accidental, shook the granite hearth's
Gray vault, untouched yet by the sun's first ray.
I looked up from the pages I'd just read,
And frost had swung the birches low to earth's
Right place for love and all that cannot stay.

On Hearing Gwendolyn Brooks
[COLUMBUS DAY, 1990]

Her voice contains a zoo of purrs and growls,
Of croons and grunts and hisses, yawps and howls.

Or maybe, it's the sound of human being
A truth volcano, patient, hearing, seeing;
Above all, elemental, like a speaking

Lava, abrasive, fluent, hotly creaking,
That rolls relentless toward a blue-eyed ocean.

The darkened soil, swept up in locomotion,
Enlarges narrow, pallid shores—its call,
A black and boiling, comprehending drawl.

Thus she, by just a whisper, or perhaps
A gasp, can smolder landscapes, widen maps.

Emily's Words

The truth must dazzle gradually
—Emily Dickinson

Unsquandered, sure and quiet as a root,
She stayed at home all dressed in pleated white,
And accurately weighed the brain of God,
The sum of acts not carried out. Unwed,
That she not be divided, she stayed whole,
And heard the sound the tooth makes in the soul.
A little knife that cuts through at a slant,
Her voice, ungendered like a child's, not meant
To chant "Our Fathers" under Sunday trees,
Unlocked a phoenix from the frozen seas.
"Called back," she wrote, the mourners treading so,
That from her gypsy face a light broke through.
She died in May, and one thing struck them all:
The coffin was astonishingly small.

Sweeping

I whisk the litter from my mother's tomb.
I do it blind, I do it in my sleep—
While dreaming to the rhythm of the broom,

The ancient, tidal motion of her womb.
I'm very good at shoring up a heap—
It quiets all the corners of the room,

Where prayers have shed the echo of their weep.
The patterns on the rug begin to bloom,
And muted shadows sing as they grow deep;

I hear the bristles breathing when I sweep.

The Old Capitalist

It's come to this: Who once ran industries
And revelled in the factory's macho din,
Preferred oak-panelled smoking rooms to trees,
Liked Spanish olives with his English gin,
Now labors with his walker through the park.
The homeless bums ignore the hierarch,

And he, in turn, pretends they don't exist.
He finds a bench not serving as a bed,
And sits there like a practiced hedonist.
Cicadas ring from branches overhead.
He listens, smiles, and calmly murmurs twice,
Not minding who will hear him, "This is nice."

The desert air's so pure, he can count seven
Layers of mountains, backed by peaks, backed by
The dreamy blue of an unending sky,
As if there were no obstacle to heaven,
Whose shares he basks in to his bones' content,
Like an inheritance he never spent.

Dividing China

Our mother had a set of Royal Doulton—
Twelve place settings—my sister counts the bowls,
While I admire the formal Rondo pattern:
Its golden chain of flourishes and scrolls
Engirdles perfect alabaster spheres,
As fair as Mother felt all life should be,
Before her own lived up to all her fears;
So now it's one for you, and one for me.

But here's a pretty lid without its dish.
We search for something missing—Broken? Lost?
Decide to split the gravy boat and platter
To even up the score. Our gibberish
Is meant to mask some qualm (unspoken cost);
Some question about squaring love with matter.

Parking Lot

It's true that billboard silhouettes and power
Pylons rebuke dusk's fair and fragile fire,
As those who go on living have to prowl
And watch for someone leaving down each aisle.
While this takes place, a tender moon dips toward
The peach and blood horizon, pale, ignored.

I try to memorize impermanence:
The strange, alarming beauty of the sky,
The white moon's path, the twilight's deep, blue eye.
I want to stay till everything makes sense.
But oily-footed pigeons flap and chase—
A red Camaro, flushing them apart,
Pulls up behind me, waiting for my space:
It glistens, mean and earthly, like a heart.

About the Author

California native Leslie Monsour was educated at Scripps College in Claremont, California, and the University of Colorado in Boulder, where she received her degree in English Literature. She has been a reference librarian at the Huntington Library in San Marino, California; a news reporter for Pacifica Radio; and a research consultant for documentaries. She has also taught Spanish Poetry at Florence Avenue Middle School in Los Angeles, and has been an instructor for the U.C.L.A. Extension Writers' Program. One of the most anthologized contemporary poets, her work has appeared in numerous journals, including *The Birmingham Poetry Review, Hellas, The Lyric, Dark Horse,* and *Poetry.* In 1998, Robert Barth published her collection, *Earth's Beauty, Desire, & Loss,* and in 1999, Aralia Press at West Chester University published a letterpress edition of her poems, *Indelibility.*